Copyright © 2022 by
Proving Press

All rights reserved.
This book, or parts thereof, may not be
reproduced in any form without permission.

Hardback ISBN: 978-1-63337-640-3
E-Book ISBN: 978-1-63337-641-0

Printed in the United States of America
1 3 5 7 9 10 8 6 4 2

To Erich- My husband, my best friend, my love, my personal dream catcher. Thank you for always encouraging me and never letting me give up. Thank you for having faith in me, for helping me to believe in myself.

To Michael- My son, my love, my inspiration, my personal kaleidoscope. Thank you for helping me see how beautiful the world is, and helping me to see it through a much different light.

I can't believe we are here again, another day in the boiling sun after another exhausting week of practice. These bleachers are ridiculously overcrowded for such a hot day, and everyone in the neighborhood seems to be here. Thank heavens it's the last game of the season.

I sit here cracking apart peanut shells, dropping the scraps to the ground below and scarfing down another handful of peanuts, hoping to eat my anxiety away. With my legs shaking nervously, I wait to watch my pride and joy take the field. I wait and I wait. I'm rattled from my thoughts by families cheering and clapping. "Let's go Cubs!" a man in sunglasses yells, followed by a lot of woo-hoos.

The crowd is getting energized as the boys and girls run out to the field for their warmup exercises. Ahh, here we go, here comes our team. I quickly start to search for Michael among all the kids in yellow T-shirts. *They are moving in a million directions, and they seem to be missing someone—my Michael. Oh geez, what happened? Where could he be?*

I frantically search THE BEES dugout and there I find him. *Oh my goodness, he's still tugging at his socks and T-shirt. He hasn't been comfortable in those the entire season.* He continues to stand in the dugout with his brows scrunched together, a frown on his face, tugging at his T-shirt. *Hmm. He's frustrated and overwhelmed, and we've only been here about forty-five minutes,* I think to myself as my heart fills with guilt. And I wonder: *Did I do the right thing? Did I push him too far too fast? Is this even helpful at all?*

After what feels like a lifetime, Michael still hasn't emerged for warmups, and I can't tell if he is even going to. *I should have known. He isn't loving this—the heat and the noise from the already-excited crowd are going to be too much for him today. Maybe we should go home.* I inch farther and farther toward the edge of my bench, wrestling mentally about whether or not to go get him and just head home or stay and try to calm my nerves. *I should gather my things.*

Just as I am about to stand up, our coach goes over in an attempt to coax him out of the dugout and into some part of today's activities. *Well, there goes Coach Carter, maybe I should wait and see what happens. Michael really likes him.* Much to my surprise, Michael goes with him despite the heat of the sun, the noise of the crowd, and his continued frustration with his uniform. *Thank goodness for Coach Carter.*

As I continue to watch the teams warm up with running, catching, and passing drills, I notice how the other kids seem to do everything with such ease. *Look at the huge smiles on their faces. They are serious and excited about the game today.*

I glue my attention to my little boy, and I vaguely listen to the chatter of the other families sweating it out with me in the stands. They share stories about how great practice was this week and how much they have enjoyed the season. *Seriously?* With my thoughts racing, I am reminded that we didn't sign up to play for the love of the game.

Michael continues to be in deep discussion with Coach Carter, who attempts to get Michael engaged in some passing and catching activities. Together they lob the ball back and forth.

A guy in a blue ball cap stretches over to share news with a friend in an orange T-shirt.

"Hey Joe, have you noticed how good Olivia has gotten at trapping the ball in her mitt?"

"Yeah, man. She has done a great job with that. Her extra practice is really paying off."

A lady in a green dress with a baby bouncing on her knee chimes in. "Spencer's running drills have really helped with his speed too. He gets up every morning and does them."

Oh, no wonder they've enjoyed the season. Their kids are having so much fun. But our experience is not quite the same as that of the other families. I don't sit here dreaming of big hits with a crack of the bat and a grand slam. I don't sit here thinking of fancy plays or acrobatic catches where children jump to snatch the ball out of mid-air, fall to the ground, roll and pop back up to make the perfect play.

I sit here, I watch, and I wonder: *Will he notice the other kids in the dugout? Maybe even talk with them? Will he stick with it today despite the heat?* There are no guarantees, so for now, all I can do is watch and pray.

To whom it concerns, be patient and kind.

Ugh, my goodness, could this day get any hotter? My skin is boiling! It's been sizzling hot, and after many innings, even the best of the best, the lovers of baseball, are beginning to show signs that the blazing sun is starting to get to them. Even the crowd, who have been loud, excited, and part of this game from the very beginning, has quieted down and settled into their positions in the stands, quenching their thirst with bottles of water and making fans out of their programs.

Despite our best efforts to stay cool, we're basically just melting. Finally, we've reached the last inning. *We've seen some fancy plays and exciting catches, though. This has been a great game. The kids have given their all, while playing through bumps and bruises and this crazy heat!*

With the smell of suntan lotion and popcorn lingering in the air, I begin to chew on my fingernail and wait for the call. *This is the last chance Michael will have to take a turn at bat.*

"NEXT BATTER—MICHAEL!" yells Coach Carter enthusiastically. With a half-hearted attempt to get comfortable, I wipe sweat from my brow and tuck a wild strand of hair back behind my ear. My heart holds onto some hope while I wait patiently, as does everyone else on his team. *Is he going to take his turn at bat this time? Is this the moment when he leaves all the stress and distractions behind him? Is this the moment when he gives it a try?*

There is a murmuring from the crowd, but it has a quiet, patient buzz to it, as it takes Michael some time to realize his coaches are trying to get him to try a turn at bat. Another call of "MICHAEL" comes from Coach Carter.

The lady in the green dress starts waving her hands and yelling, "Come on, Michael. It's your turn, buddy."

And then Joe in the orange T-shirt screams, "You can do it!" while clapping wildly.

Suddenly there's movement in the dugout, a few more minutes pass, and Michael emerges. My chest tightens and my heart does a silent fist pump. *YES! He's going to give it a try. This **is** the moment.* He walks to home plate dragging his baseball bat behind him, his oversized helmet shaking and a great big smile on his face.

To whom it concerns, be uplifting and a believer in others.

In high spirits he yells, "It's my turn, Mom!" I smile at my pride and joy and try to catch my breath.

"Great job, buddy! I knew you could do it!" I reply in a strangled voice.

I crack open the last water bottle I have to try to quench my thirst. *He has achieved so much in that short journey to the plate.* Coach Carter helps to orient him in front of the catcher.

"Ok, buddy, hold the bat out by your shoulder just like we practiced this week. And put your feet to this side of the plate." Everyone continues to wait patiently. Taking a sip of my water I wonder, *Do they know how difficult this is for him?* I take a deep breath and I briefly close my eyes to pray.

"Hey Jackson!" yells the coach from the Cubs. Everyone turns their attention to the coach for the other team. He makes eye contact with the young boy who is pitching, and he motions with his hands for the pitcher to creep forward.

"Umm…wait a minute," I mumble under my breath. *What's happening? Is he trying to give Michael a better chance to hit the ball? Crouching down slightly, the tension mounts in the pit of my stomach as I worry. Are they mad? Did they notice? I can't believe the coach just did that. What is everyone going to think?*

I quickly scan the stands and listen carefully to the crowd generating some small talk while they wait. *Well it doesn't seem like anybody is upset. They all seem fine. Surely they saw what happened.*

The pitcher raises his eyebrows in surprise, gives a gentle nod, and sneaks forward. He winds up and lets the ball fly. Whoosh!

Michael loosely swings and…misses. "STRRRRIKKKKE ONE!" yells the umpire.

I take a deep breath, clap until my hands are sore, and scream, "You almost had it! Good job!" Once again, Coach Carter helps him get oriented and the other coach continues to encourage the pitcher to creep forward bit by bit. *Huh? What's happening?* With no rest from the heat, I'm suddenly flooded with a bizarre mix of emotions: I'm self-conscious but extremely proud that he has stayed with it today and is giving it a try.

Clearly everyone can see Jackson is much closer to Michael than he should be. I quickly scan the crowd again for any signs of frustration or anger from the families. I shrug. *Still seems like a bunch of small talk to me. No one seems to care at all.* Speechless, I sit a little taller on my bench, my worries slowly starting to fall to the ground like the peanut shells.

The young boy pitching adjusts his cap to make himself more comfortable. He's clearly been playing for years. He winds up and lets another ball fly. Whoosh!

In that brief moment, Michael looks up to find me in the stands. He kindly gives me a thumbs up. *Aww....he wants me to know he's okay. I can't believe he is enjoying this so much.* However, in that split second of distraction, the ball flies right by him with no swing whatsoever. Surprised by the ball passing him, he jumps backward and drops his bat to the ground.

Aaugh!

"STRRRRIKKKKE TWO!" yells the umpire as he briefly paces back and forth at the base.

My eyes welling up with tears, I start to panic. *No. No. No.... You can't do this now. You need to help him.* I pull myself together as quickly as I can.

"Michael, look at me, buddy!" I shout in a tremulous voice and sit up as tall as I can. "You can do it. Everything is okay." Coach Carter helps Michael dust off his shoes in an attempt to help calm him. With his shoulders back and his chin lifted high, Michael screams in a high-pitched voice as he points at his cleats. "It's okay, Mom! They're clean!"

Phew.

The lady in the green dress leans back to give me an encouraging smile. "He's doing amazing."

I needed that. With my heart in my throat, I choke out a simple, "It's a good day."

Out of the corner of my eye I get a glimpse of Michael's teammates lining the edge of their dugout. A low whisper changes into chants of encouragement from both teams. The murmuring from the crowd bubbles over with clapping and cheering. Astonished by his willingness to be a part of the game, they encourage him with "You've got this!" and "Give it another try!"

Once again, Coach Carter helps him get ready. "Put your feet back by the base," he says as he guides Michael to where he needs to be. "Hold your bat up above your shoulder and watch the ball when he tosses it," he stresses. The pitcher is encouraged to creep forward one more time, and I take another chance to pray.

To whom it concerns, be supportive and compassionate.

This time the young boy generously calls out, "Michael, here it comes!" He gives a slight pause to make sure he has Michael's attention and sends the last ball gently cruising through the air. Whoosh!

WHACK!!!!

HE DID IT! HE REALLY DID IT! HE HIT THE BALL! The crowd bursts with excitement, and there he stands, staring at me with that same huge smile on his flushed face.

Everyone is yelling for him to run. I spring to my feet, wildly gesturing toward the plate. I screech, " Go to first base!" He figures it out and gives me a thumbs up. He trots off toward the base, dragging his bat behind him, in no hurry. *Look at that grin!* My heart swells and I savor this moment. *He is having a great time.*

THUMP!

Somehow he manages to make a hop onto first base in glorious fashion before the ball can get there, despite his *what's the hurry?* pace. The umpire calls "SAFE!" as he swipes his arms from side to side.

Caught in the moment, I stomp my feet with excitement and wail, "Woo-hoo! Way to go, Michael! Great job!"

The man in the blue ball cap flings his hands up and yells, "That a boy!" Meanwhile, several of Michael's teammates do their own celebrations: fist bumps, high fives, and bouncing up and down. Shaking, I slowly sit back down on the bleachers and gulp down most of my water. *He did it, he really did it. He kept trying even though it was hard.*

Alarm bells start ringing in my ears as I notice the next batter emerging from the Bees dugout. *You've got to be kidding me. Why? Why does our fastest runner have to be the one following Michael?* The excitement dies down when the next batter approaches the plate and gets ready for his turn at bat.

"Knock it out of the park, Trey!" a proud papa shouts as the boy at bat gets set in his stance.

In the time it takes him to step up to the base after a few practice swings, Michael loses focus on the game and the crowd and starts to wander around. Coach Carter tries to get him to stay on or near the base as the game continues on. "Michael, stay right there. Keep your foot on the base, buddy."

Michael has never made it to the bases before, not even in practice. I bite my lip in an attempt to contain my worry. He isn't even paying attention to the game anymore. Now I sit, I watch, and I wonder. Will he know what to do if the next batter hits the ball? Will he run? Is he going to know that he needs to run to the next base, or will he run to the field? Will he just stay there on first base? There is no way to know, so there I sit with my heart pounding in my chest and sweat dripping from my temples.

Is this how the other families feel watching their kids? Are they confident that their kid can make the play or do they fill up with anxiety as they wait to see what happens? Butterflies dance around in my stomach as I wait. The suspense is killing me, but I am so proud of him.

Crack!!!

I'm startled out of my thoughts as I hear the ball hitting the bat. The batter races off with arms and legs pumping as hard as he can. "Come on, Michael. Come on, buddy! Run to the next base!" Coach Carter bellows while gesturing toward second base. Michael lights up the field with a smile as he acknowledges his coach. And quick as a snail, Michael starts to **walk** toward second base.

"Bwahaha!" Bursting out with a hearty chuckle, Coach Carter attempts to run backward, trying to urge Michael to pick up his pace. "Don't let me get there before you, Mike!" he yells, clearly as excited for Michael as everyone else. Sweating and stumbling together they tap second base and… keep on going!

Oh my goodness! They aren't slowing down. He can't be serious. Taking advantage of the opportunity of having Michael engaged in the game, Coach Carter tries to get him to go all the way to third base. "Come on, buddy. We can get to the next one!" Nervously, I bite down on what is left of my last fingernail. I rock back and forth a little bit as I frantically glance from what they are doing to what is happening in the field.

"Teehee-hee." I cover my mouth to stifle my own laughter as Michael takes up a faster scamper. "He really wants to beat Coach Carter," I mumble as if telling a secret. Together they land on third base, gasping with relief that they've made it.

"Great job. You did it." Coach Carter holds up his hand to collect a high five from Michael, and then he has to shake it off after Michael winds up and swings harder for the high five than he did to hit the ball with the bat.

As the players all settle into their current positions, Coach Carter wipes the sweat off his neck with his handkerchief and makes his way back to first base to help the player waiting there. Without a cloud to be found in the sky, the heat continues to beat down and the crowd becomes calm again as we all wait for the next player to step up to home plate.

Yuck, that's so gross. I pull away the clump of hair that is sticking to my face, irritated with the sweat that's dripping down my back while I wait for the next batter. She quickly comes bounding out of the dugout toward the infield. *Aww, I like her. She is such a sweetheart.* After a couple of misses, she barely hits the ball with the tip of her bat and sends it off toward third.

"Oh no! Oh no! OH NO! MICHAEL, LOOK OUT!" I yell.

She takes off running to first and Trey slides his way into second. Both are safe at their bases and are signaled by the coaches to stay where they are. And Michael…is crouching down inspecting whatever is **under** third base. He looks up to find me in the stands. "It's okay, Mom. I'll put it back."

Shoot, he has completely lost interest in the game. He didn't move at all. Was he supposed to? Sigh. *I don't even know what he's supposed to do, so how is he supposed to know?* And just like that, I am a bundle of nerves again. I do the only thing I know to do at this point and start listening to the crowd. Maybe they'll say something that gives me a clue.

Well, they're chatting about their weekend...that's not helpful. And they're talking about the heat...again, not helpful. I shake my head. *Did they notice he didn't move? Do they even care? Everyone seems to be jabbering about how the kids are doing or the heat. So I guess they are all still okay with things.*

Inhaling deeply, I listen in on one more conversation. "Yes, the bases are loaded. We have a good chance of winning now."

Oh, that's a good point. I let that sink in, and I pray as it dawns on me that he *MUST* run.

To whom it concerns, be loving and accepting.

Feeling out of place, I turn my thoughts back to Michael. *How do I let him know that he needs to run to the next base? He has to move, but he's too far away for me to get his attention. I don't know how to help him from here.* In a panic, I search my surroundings looking for some way to get close enough to him.

Everything is too far away. Nope...right there! There's a spot in the bleachers on the third base line. In a knee-jerk reaction, I hastily gather everything I have with me, determined to race over to the bleachers by third base before someone can steal my spot. I'm just about to bolt out of there when I see them: a mom and daughter coming back with popcorn and drinks. *Well, that explains the open seats in all of this chaos.*

Thud!

I gasp as I flop back down on the bleachers. The man in the blue hat turns around to check on me. "You okay?"

"Yes," I sheepishly reply. "I was just going to move closer to Michael, but someone seems to have the seat."

"Ah, well, I'm not sure you would have made it."

He's right. I don't have enough time to get there. If I move, he will lose me in the crowd. I don't want him to panic; things have been so good. At this point I am absolutely helpless, so all I can do is continue to nervously shake my leg and watch Michael carefully.

"Excuse me," says the elderly gentleman next to me, "but do you know what is so interesting under the base?"

I *giggle. Michael's got everyone else wondering now.* I smile proudly and shrug my shoulders. "I have no idea." *I really don't know what's so interesting under the base, but he looks pretty happy.*

Coach Carter, realizing where he is needed most for the upcoming play, makes his way back to Michael. *Ah-ha, there we go. Coach Carter will help him, and that means I don't have to go running across the field like a crazy woman.* With a big smile on his face and his big booming voice he says, "Hey Mike. We're getting ready to run to home plate. You're almost done, bud. Hang in there." Coach Carter takes a minute to listen to what Michael has to say about the curious world under the base, and then he helps him put it back on the ground. Michael looks up to find me in the crowd.

Thank heavens I didn't move. I wave at him cheerfully so he knows I am watching. He returns my wave with two thumbs-up, telling me that he is still having a good time. Coach Carter steps back and Michael tries to pick up the base, again peeking into the curious unknown world. *Yep, thank goodness for Coach Carter.*

Jackson strikes out our next two batters, and the tension of the game revs the crowd back up as they begin shouting and trying to cheer on their players. "It's the bottom of the ninth, let's finish strong, Bees!" shouts the man in the orange T-shirt. "Strike this last player out, Jackson!"

Ah yes, this is the moment for which players who love the game wait. The bases are loaded, and it's a chance to be the hero.

Emerging from the dugout is our last chance to get our runners home. *You've got to be kidding me. It's Maggie, and she's a power hitter. This is it. He has to be ready to move. There is no other choice. She'll hit the ball, she always does. They're going to run him over if he stays there.* The shaking of my legs has gone into overdrive, and I fan my face rapidly like a plane ready to take off. *Man, everyone would hate me if they knew that some part of me just wants the girl to strike out. I don't think my heart or stomach can take any more, and he's already done so much today.*

Maggie steps up to the base, taps the bat on the ground three times, places it into her swing position, and waits for the pitch with a wide-eyed look on her face and a broad grin to match her confidence. KA-BOOM! She blasts the ball into the outfield. The ball flies over the outfielder's head and rebounds off the wall. And just like that, lickety split, she immediately makes her way to first base. Trey looks like he's been shot out of a cannon as he starts pumping his way to third. The outfielder collects the ball and tosses it back to the second baseman.

My love, still very interested in what's going on under third base, doesn't realize that the next batter has sent everything into motion again. In the middle of all the hubbub, Coach Carter tries to get Michael to move. "Hey Mike, don't let me beat you to home plate!" he yells and starts his backward jog toward home, but this time Michael isn't ready to go and doesn't care about racing.

All the while, with arms and legs still pumping, Trey comes racing toward third and realizes Michael has not moved. Wide eyed and stunned, he shouts, "Michael GO! GO! GO!"

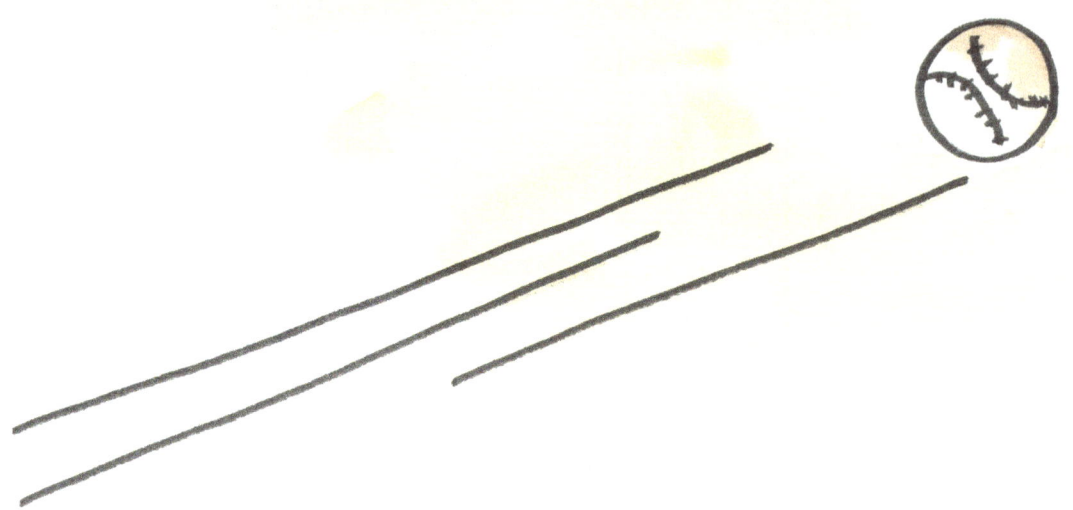

Startled out of his curiosity, Michael sees Trey coming. He jumps up suddenly and freezes. He stands motionless, staring at Trey without blinking. *It's all too much. Everything is happening too fast for him. He doesn't know what to do.* With my eyes welling up with tears, I scream, "You gotta run, buddy! Run to the next base!"

Trey watches as the coach urges them both to move on toward home. Realizing Michael isn't moving, Trey grabs Michael's hand and off to home base they go as a team. I am surrounded by the beautiful noise of everyone cheering on the two runners. Trey slows down to run with Michael, pointing to home plate. "Run to that base, Mike. Come on, you can do it!" In what feels like a lifetime for me, I watch and pray as everything seems to happen in slow motion.

To whom it concerns, be positive and inspiring.

The outfielder throws the ball to the player on second base, who throws it to the catcher at home plate just as the two runners are arriving. The ball falls just a couple of steps to the side of the base, right into the catcher's mitt. With one quick grasp, he has the ball. *Oh no!* My pounding heart starts to deflate. *All he has to do is touch the base and Michael will be out.* Wildly I jump up and down, screaming, "Keep going, Michael! You can do it!"

This time Michael doesn't hop onto the plate with excitement. His eyes are still wide, running as fast as his legs can carry him. Just as he steps on the base, the catcher stretches in to step on the plate.

"SAFE!" the umpire shouts and waves his arms to show that Michael made it.

He made it! He made it! HE MADE IT! Throwing a fist pump into the air, jumping and clapping excitedly just like the other families, I am caught up in the game. "YES! HE DID IT! GREAT JOB, MICHAEL!"

The lady in the green dress turns around to share in our joy. "This really has been a good day for you guys," she says with a smile. I nod a silent yes while fighting back the happy tears.

I stand motionless with my hands over my heart, completely stunned as I watch the celebration in front of me. Players and coaches from both teams congratulate Michael. Patting him on the back with a, "You did it, big guy" and "Great job."

He has no idea why they are so happy with him, but I love that smile. It's been an amazing day. Beaming with pride, I am once again reminded that we didn't sign up to play for the love of the game. *They have no idea what he has accomplished today, but they are cheering him on even though he did it very differently and needed more help.*

And just like that, the game has come to an end. The two teams are scattering, making their separate ways toward their families and the snack tables. I gather my trash, my bag, and my empty water bottles. *I don't know much about baseball, but this has been awesome.* Feeling on top of the world, I make my way out of the stands to go find my Michael, just as a gentle breeze finally blows across the field. *Sweet relief. I can breathe again.*

As I approach the team, I hear Coach Carter giving Michael praise while handing him a certificate for his efforts today. "We are so proud of you for trying. We know it was hard, but you stuck with it and did a great job." I stand back and wait, watching as Michael's teammates continue with the pats on the back, the high fives and fist bumps. *And that's why we signed up to play.*

They congratulate him for a "great game" as juice boxes and fruit snacks are passed out to the hungry, thirsty bunch of players. *Aww, look at that smile.* But everything is still happening too fast. Too much movement, too much noise, and too many people talking to him at the same time. *Let him handle it.* By the time the last teammate celebrates with him, he can barely get the word "thanks" out.

I don't know who really won the game or what happened with the other runners, but I silently celebrate that moment with pride in my heart for Michael's achievements— achievements that for us, had very little to do with baseball.

I'm desperate to know what he thought of his day. I wait a few minutes as the buzz of the crowd around Michael shifts their focus elsewhere. As he quietly collects his snacks and juice, he studies the large number of people nearby, carefully plans his exit from the crowd, then decides to walk around them to make his way toward me.

He comes trotting over to me with his bat dragging behind him, a juice box in his *hand, and that big, beautiful smile on his face like he has just had the time of his life. And to think I thought signing him up for baseball was a bad idea. Maybe he would like to give it another try next season.* He hands me his "Player of the Game" certificate and begins to dig into the fruit snacks, trying to avoid the yellow ones.

"Hey buddy, I am very proud of you. You did so much today. Did you have fun?"

"Yep," he replies with a smile.

"Well, what do you think about trying baseball again next season?"

"No thanks. I'll try something else."

And that was the end of baseball, but not the end of a memory that will stay with me a lifetime. So I'll take the opportunity to pause and pray once more…

About the Author:

I am a wife, a mother and a teacher of 20+ years. I am a first time author, trying to follow a dream that I have had since my childhood. So this is a long time coming. With the push of my wonderful husband I have made an attempt to go further on this journey than I ever really thought I could. I hope you find this book both meaningful, relatable and even a bit humorous as our journeys can often be.

POWER OF WORDS

One of the most powerful weapons we have in society is the spoken or written word. Words can be strong and build up another or words can be powerful and hurtful. The words we choose impact a great many people around us. The biggest influence of our words determines how our children see the world. Do we use our words to build up their innocence, beauty and love for one another? -Lia-Mae Kass.

www.ingramcontent.com/pod-product-compliance
Lightning Source LLC
LaVergne TN
LVHW070949070426
835507LV00030B/3467